The Southern Cotswolds

A little souvenir

CHRIS ANDREWS PUBLICATIONS LTD

Stroud

Also available in this series:

The Cotswolds North
Stratford upon Avon
Oxford
Bath
Cheltenham
Henley on Thames
Cambridge
London
The Chilterns
The Peak District
Guernsey
Sark
Alderney

For information on all our publications please see

www.cap-ox.co.uk

The Cotswolds

INTRODUCTION

For some the name "Cotswolds" conjures a picture of sheltered valleys harbouring villages of honey coloured stone nestling beside clear, fast flowing streams. Others may see the high, bleak open countryside criss-crossed by dry stone walls, or perhaps the bustling old market towns with their fine perpendicular churches. All these views are united by stone; it is oolitic limestone that has created the underlying landscape of the Cotswolds and the buildings for which the area is famed.

Early evidence of stonemasonry can be seen over the whole Cotswolds, including the long barrow at Uley, a fine example of skilfully constructed dry stone walls in an area known for the quality and hue of its stone.

The Romans established a military zone in the Cotswolds, serviced by routes built with stone, some of those remaining are still followed by today's highways. A grass grown amphitheatre and a museum of Roman treasures remind us of the importance of the market town of Cirencester in former times. The Anglo Saxons left little evidence of their rule, other than a legacy of place-

names and a few stone churches tucked away in quiet valleys, such as that in the tiny hamlet of Coln Rogers

Following the Norman conquest of 1066 the church increased in power and wealth, built upon a thriving wool industry. By Domesday in 1086, most of the present day villages existed and an open field system had been created, with vast flocks of sheep grazing on the open sheep walk.

Today's market towns, such as Cirencester or Winchcombe, were founded at this time, built of local stone with the help of masonry skills brought with the Normans. By the 15th century the whole country was so dependent on the wool industry that the Lord Chancellor's seat in the House of Lords came to be known as the woolsack.

Cotswold stone houses at Duntisbourne Leer

Lechlade and the Thames

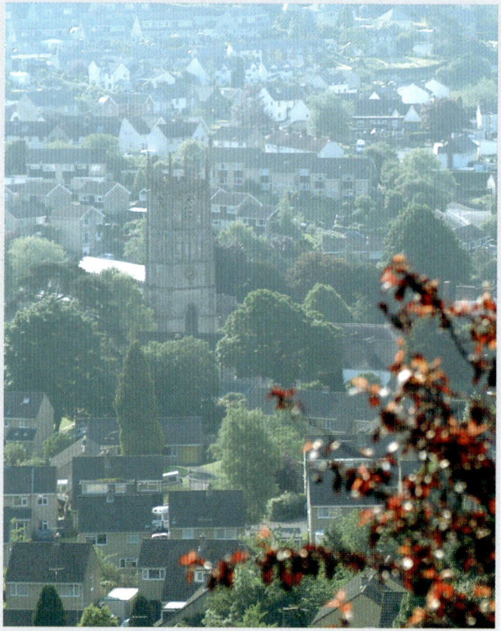

The Cotswolds thrived upon the wool trade; wealthy merchants built fine houses and elegant perpendicular churches. Wool processing became increasingly important to the economy; it was initially a cottage industry, but during the 16th century the weaving and fulling became concentrated in the towns and villages of the western Cotswolds where the fast flowing streams from the steep slopes powered the mills.

Between 1700 and 1840, parliamentary intervention, higher taxation and an increase in wool production elsewhere, led to a decline in the Cotswold wool

 Wotton-under-Edge

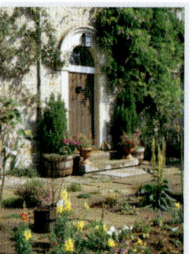

industry and the area paid for an over reliance on the trade. Ironically the rich legacy of 15th and 16th century buildings we see today is partly due to this period of poverty, as there was little money available for new building, although a wealthy minority did build several substantial country houses.

The Cotswolds today reflect their interesting and varied past, and the efforts of many to preserve and maintain their atmosphere. The whole area is designated one of Outstanding Natural Beauty and this little book attempts to show something of its charm. This volume shows the area from the southern edge to the centre, a sister publication "The Cotswolds North" covers the centre to the northern boundary.

Witney Church

12 Church Green, Witney

Village pond and houses at dawn, Westwell

14 Minster Lovell Hall

Haymaking in late summer fields

16 Minster Lovell, Ablington,

Coln St Aldwyns and Barnsley

18 Ploughing Championships at Filkins

20 Eastleach Turville

Eastleach Martin, the church and River Leach

22 Coln St Denis

Winson

26 Cotswold roads in the Coln Valley

The hunt meet at Bibury Court

Arlington Row, Bibury

30 Cotswold Cottages at Bibury

The Coln at Bibury

32 Thames bridge at Lechlade

Thames Head statue at St John's Lock Lechlade

34 Fairford Church

The stained glass in Fairford Church is one of the finest complete sets of glass in England

36 Cirencester Church and The Abbey Grounds

38 Roman mosaic in the Corinium museum, Cirencester

Near the source of The Thames at Kemble

Cirecester open air pool and the backs of Cecily Hill houses

42 The Duntisbourne valley

Characteristic Cotswold stone cottages at Bisley

44 Painswick, the town showing the characteristic 'white' Cotswold stone of the area

Painswick churchyard

46 Stroud from the south

The Severn Vale from Selsley Common, Stroud

48　St Cyr, Stonehouse and the Canal

50   The Woolpack at Slad, frequented and immortalised by Laurie Lee

Minchinhampton

54　Owlpen Manor

Fruit and veg at Dursley

60 Dursley

Victoria Jubilee Clock and the High Street, Wottton under Edge

62 Tetbury

First published 2005, revised and updated 2014

by

Chris Andrews Publications Ltd 15 Curtis Yard North Hinksey Lane Oxford OX2 0NA

Telephone: +44(0)1865 723404 email: chris.andrews1@btclick.com Photos by Chris Andrews, Angus Palmer

ISBN 1 905385 04 8 All material © Chris Andrews Publications
ISBN 978 1 905385 04 1

www.cap-ox.com

All rights reserved. No part of this publication may be reproduced, stored in a retrieval system, or transmitted, in any form or by any means, without prior permission of the copyright holder. The right of Chris Andrews as author of this work have been asserted by him in accordance with the Copyright, Designs and Patents Act 1988.

Front Cover: Arlington Row, Bibury Title page: Cotswold cat This page: Cotswold lambs Back cover: Cheltenham

Chris Andrews

Chris Andrews work is known throughout England and the Channel Islands, and is seen in a variety of publications including calendars, posters, fine art prints and books.

This 'Little Souvenir' series attempts to show something of the unique charm of the Cotswolds Area of Outstanding Natural Beauty in an attractive and portable form

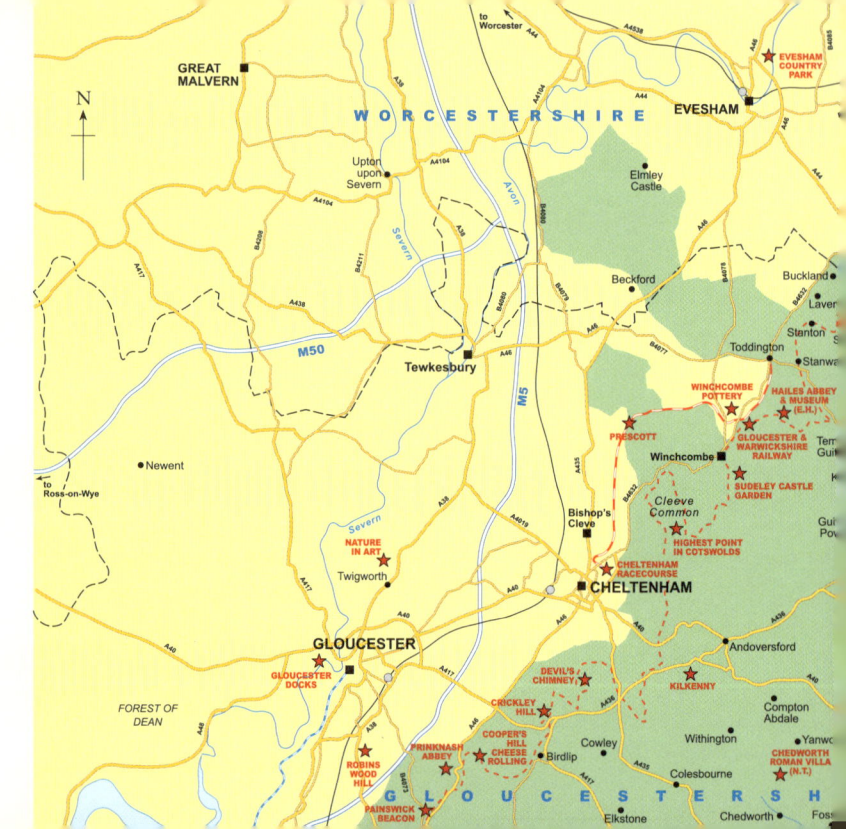